Introduction

Several years ago, when we hired a new CEO for our ministry, he had every member of our staff read a particular book about change. He did this because the vast majority of people resist change; they fear it. For many people, change is a difficult, painful, and labor-intensive process. They think it takes a huge amount of effort to change their thoughts, actions, and circumstances.

Do you keep experiencing the same challenges and failures in your life? Are you believing for a breakthrough in the areas of healing, finances, or deliverance but aren't seeing results? Do you know what God's calling is for your life, but you just don't see how to get there?

What if I told you that you can change your life effortlessly? The key to seeing God's will manifest in your life—in your body, bank account, business, relationships, and more—is by sowing God's Word into your heart. It's just that simple!

In this booklet, I want to share with you some truths from the Word of God that can totally transform the way you understand and approach change. If you receive these truths into your heart and apply them to your life, you'll be able to see change effortlessly take place in your life. I've watched this happen time and again in my own life and through the lives of others touched by this ministry.

Maybe you suspect there's something more to your life. You have dreams. You have desires. You look at where you are, and it's not satisfying. You know there's got to be something more, but, you're afraid to change. I want to tell you that there is more because God said He will give you the desires of your heart (Ps. 37:4).

The Word of God is the incorruptible seed (1 Pet. 1:23) that, when sown into the soil of your heart, will yield an abundant harvest (Mark 4:20). If you want to see change outwardly, it has to begin on the inside by sowing the Word of God. If you can just change the way you think—the way you are on the inside—then you'll see a change in your life. And your life will change effortlessly!

Effortless Change

Andrew Wommack

Effortless
Change

Andrew Wommack

Published in partnership between Andrew Wommack Ministries and Harrison House Publishers.

Woodland Park, CO 80863 – Shippensburg, PA 17257

ISBN 13 TP: 978-1-59548-651-6

For Worldwide Distribution, Printed in the USA

1 2 3 4 5 6 / 26 25 24 23

Contents

Do Things Differently

For we dare not make ourselves of the number, or compare ourselves with some that commend themselves: but they measuring themselves by themselves, and comparing themselves among themselves, are not wise.

2 Corinthians 10:12

In my meetings, one of the things that I'll ask people is if they know that there's more to life than what they're currently experiencing. Nearly every hand in the place will go up. Then I'll ask, "How many of you want to change your life and see things differently?" Again, most people raise their hands because they want a change. That is huge!

Do you need change in your health, marriage, finances, career, or some other area in your life? Maybe you've felt dissatisfied with just getting up, going to work, coming home, and going back to bed. If so, you've got to start doing something differently. The truth is that God has more for you, but you can't keep doing the same things that got you to where you are. I've heard that the definition of insanity is to keep doing the same thing and expecting different results.

The vast majority of people who come to our meetings are born again. Many of them are already baptized in the Holy Spirit. These are people who love God, are seeking Him, and desiring change. If you are similar to the people who come to our meetings, you may recognize a need for change. But are you going to do something different?

The Bible teaches that, in the same way you plant a seed, God has given you a system through His Word to change your life for the better. A seed doesn't travail, it doesn't groan, and it doesn't go through pain. When you see an apple, you know the tree didn't labor to produce it. It's just the nature of a seed to grow into a tree and then produce fruit. I believe that the Word of God will change your life in the same way.

Most people look around to gauge the average life experience. They see that the average person is sick, poor, and their emotions are up and down like a yo-yo. They compare themselves to others, which isn't wise (2 Cor. 10:12). They live a substandard life and think, *Well, this is just the way it is with everybody else.* I'm here to tell you that God made you for more than what you are experiencing.

Don't Think Small

You may have heard me talk about the night the Lord really touched my life on March 23, 1968, but I believe the second most important day in the history of this ministry was January 31, 2002.

Our ministry and Bible college were growing, we were touching people's lives, and we were no longer struggling financially. But the Lord was calling me to do more.

We had been on television for two years at that point, but we were only reaching a small percentage of the U.S. market. Our Charis Bible College was cramped for space in a 14,600-square-foot facility. We had grown to the point that things were different than they had been, but it just seemed like we had plateaued. That was when the Lord spoke to me from Psalm 78:41.

Yea, they turned back and tempted God, and limited the Holy One of Israel.

God showed me that I was limiting Him through my small thinking. There are a number of reasons for that, but one of the primary reasons was that I had grown comfortable after years of struggling. I was just complacent. After more than thirty years in ministry, it looked like we were finally going to make it. We were seeing light at the end of the tunnel, and it wasn't another train!

Some people come up with any excuse to not follow God's plans for their lives. People will come up to me at meetings and say, "I believe God told me to attend Charis Bible College, but…," and then they give me a list of reasons why they can't do it. My response is typically, "Well, I hear what you're saying, but you lost me once you said, 'God told me.'" You see, I made a decision a long time ago that I was going to follow God's will for my life and do whatever it takes, even if it harelips the devil!

On February 11, 2002, less than two weeks after God revealed to me that I was limiting Him through my small thinking, I called my staff together—which was about two dozen people at the time—and shared with them what the Lord had showed me. I told them, "I don't know how long it will take to change this image on the inside of me, but I am going to change." I didn't know if would take a week, a month, or a year, but I was committed to changing! (We'll come back to this story later.)

Known by Your Fruit

Ye shall know them by their fruits. Do men gather grapes of thorns, or figs of thistles? Even so every good tree bringeth forth good fruit; but a corrupt tree bringeth forth evil fruit. A good tree cannot bring forth evil fruit, neither can a corrupt tree bring forth good fruit. Every tree that bringeth not forth good fruit is hewn down, and cast into the fire. Wherefore by their fruits ye shall know them.

Matthew 7:16–20

If I came over to your house to see your garden, I could tell what you planted, even though I wasn't present when you did it. All I'd have to do is observe the plants that are growing up. If you have corn growing there, you planted corn. If there are peas, you sowed peas.

You may claim that someone else came in and planted something in your garden that you did not intend. But it's ultimately your responsibility to guard and protect your garden. Whatever is growing there is what you've planted or what you've allowed to be planted.

Likewise, whatever is growing in your life is what you planted there or allowed someone else to plant in you. The direction of your life on the outside reflects your dominant way of thinking on the inside. Instead of looking for a change to take place externally in everybody and everything else around you, the first thing you need to do is recognize that change begins on the inside of you. This occurs according to the knowledge you have of God (2 Pet. 1:2–3).

God's Word is true. As you think in your heart, so are you (Prov. 23:7). This is a law of God. We cannot consistently operate differently than what we believe in our hearts. Therefore, our dominant actions are a window into our hearts. And if we want to change our actions, we have to change our hearts first. Anything less is just behavior modification and not true change.

Romans 8:6 confirms this truth:

For to be carnally minded is death; but to be spiritually minded is life and peace.

Carnal-mindedness doesn't just tend toward death—it equals death. And spiritual-mindedness doesn't just tend toward life—it equals life. I don't have to be with a person to see what they have been thinking. All I have to do is see the fruit of that person's life, and I can tell. It's like looking at a person's garden; what grows there is what was planted there.

Death is much more than just physical, where our souls and spirits depart from our bodies (James 2:26). Sickness, depression, anger, poverty, and anything else that is a result of sin are forms of death (Rom. 6:23).

You Are Complete in Him

You can pray, beg God, and get other people to intercede for you all you want. They could even lay hands on you until they rub all the hair off the top of your head, but you aren't going to see change in your life externally until you change internally.

When you got born again, God put everything on the inside of you that you will ever need. In the spirit realm, you are complete (Col. 2:10). You are as complete and perfect in the spirit realm as Jesus is.

Herein is our love made perfect, that we may have boldness in the day of judgment: because as [Jesus] is, so are we in this world.

1 John 4:17

And because ye are sons, God hath sent forth the Spirit of his Son into your hearts, crying, Abba, Father.

Galatians 4:6

In your born-again spirit, you already have all of the fruit of the Spirit: *"love, joy, peace, longsuffering, gentleness, goodness, faith, meekness, temperance"* (Gal. 5:22–23). You also have the anointing of God (1 John 2:20) and the faith of God (Gal. 2:20). Everything that you will ever have in eternity is already in you in your spirit.

There is nothing negative in your born-again spirit—no fear, unforgiveness, or unbelief. Your spirit is perfect (Heb. 12:23). But you've got to draw out what's inside by planting the seed of God's Word! But it's not the seed itself that does the work.

You see, an apple seed doesn't produce an apple tree. The apple seed activates the ground, and out of the ground comes the tree because *"the earth bringeth forth fruit of herself"* (Mark 4:28). The seed somehow takes the nutrients that are in the ground; then out of the ground comes an apple tree, and then it produces apples. This process was God's intent from the beginning.

> *And the earth brought forth grass,* and *herb yielding seed after his kind, and the tree yielding fruit, whose seed* was *in itself, after his kind: and God saw that* it was *good.*
>
> Genesis 1:12

I've seen people hold up an apple seed, and say, "Anybody can count the number of seeds in an apple, but nobody can count the number of apples in a seed." They're saying if you plant a seed, it will produce a tree that will produce hundreds of apples, and in each apple, there are many seeds, and so on. I understand the point they're making, but according to Genesis 1:11–12 and Mark 4:28, seeds don't produce apples. The earth produces the apples. The seed activates what is already in the soil—the heart.

What exactly is the heart of man? Is it your spirit or your soul? The heart is a combination of the spirit and soul. In the biblical sense, it is the very center of a person. The spirit and the soul were made to function as one. When this happens, you start to experience victory in your life. Knowing what the heart is can apply to every area of your life.

Begin to Produce

And he said, So is the kingdom of God, as if a man should cast seed into the ground; and should sleep, and rise night and day, and the seed should spring and grow up, he knoweth not how. For the earth bringeth forth fruit of herself; first the blade, then the ear, after that the full corn in the ear.

Mark 4:26–28

Just like the seed releases the power in the ground, God created His Word to release the power in our hearts. The ground doesn't care what type of seed is planted; it will just start the growth process. Likewise, our hearts don't choose to only release the power in God's Word. Any word planted in our hearts will begin to produce, which is why we need to be very selective about what we let in our hearts.

Whatever is growing in the garden of your life is what you've planted or allowed to be planted in your heart. Before you can really see change, you must do something different like quit using excuses and blaming everybody else for what is wrong in your life. You have to stop saying, "It's just fate," or "I have bad luck," or "Nothing ever works for me." Scripture reveals that as you think in your heart, that's the way you're going to be (Prov. 23:7). If you think spiritually minded, your thoughts will produce life and peace (Rom. 8:6).

In Mark 4:28, *"of herself"* is translated from the Greek word *automatos.*[1] It's where we get our English word *automatic*. The ground just produces fruit automatically. Likewise, our hearts are made to automatically produce whatever seed we sow in them. Notice that the earth is spoken of as being feminine. It has everything it needs to produce fruit except seed, or sperm.

Being born again, not of corruptible seed, but of incorruptible, by the word of God, which liveth and abideth for ever.

1 Peter 1:23

The Greek word for *seed* there is *spora*,[2] which is a derivative of the Greek word *sperma*.[3] It's saying that the Word of God is like a seed—a sperm—and it has to be planted in your heart to conceive. I talk to people all the time who pray and believe for God to do something in their lives but remain frustrated with the results. It's because they are missing the seeds of conception; they just don't know God's Word. To conceive and give birth from your spirit, you must first plant God's Word like a seed in your heart.

God's kingdom operates by laws, like the laws that govern the fruit-bearing process of a seed. And this is precisely the reason most people don't see God's best come to pass in their lives. They think that since God loves them, He will just grant their request regardless of whether they put the seed of His Word to work or not.

Conceive Your Miracle

We would think a person is absolutely crazy if they just prayed for a child but never had a relationship with someone. There was only one virgin birth, and there's not going to be another! A seed has to be planted in the womb for someone to be able to conceive and bring forth a child.

In the natural realm, we understand that. But when it comes to spiritual things, there are people who are praying for God's will to come to pass in their lives, but they aren't planting the seed of God's Word. I've had people come to me before seeking healing, and I ask, "What scripture are you standing on? What word have you put in your heart that is going to bring forth healing?" Often, people will respond, "Well, doesn't it say someplace in the Bible—I can't remember if it's the Old Testament or the New Testament—that 'by His stripes we're healed?'"

They don't even know if it's from the Old or New Covenant, but they know it's someplace in the Bible. They couldn't find 1 Peter 2:24 if they tried! I'll tell you, a person has to have a little more intimacy with the Word of God than that if they want to conceive God's best in their life.

That's like a woman just saying, "Well, is standing close to a man enough to get pregnant? Is just having him smile at me enough to get pregnant?" The truth is conception cannot take place without first planting the seed. God has already done His part: He has given us the seed of His Word! You just need to sow that Word in your heart.

For example, the Lord doesn't give us money directly. Deuteronomy 8:18 says that the Lord gives us power to get wealth. The power is in His promises—His Word. As we plant those promises in our hearts, the truth of His Word germinates, and prosperity comes.

There are many people who pray and believe for God to do something in their lives but remain frustrated with the results. It's because they are missing the seeds of conception; they don't know God's Word. To conceive and give birth from your spirit, you must first plant God's Word like a seed in your heart.

I can't tell you how important it is that you know God's Word and that you plant that seed in your heart. It could mean the difference between prosperity and poverty, or even life and death. But the seed can do nothing without soil. Scientists have actually taken seeds found at ancient historical sites and planted them. Once those seeds that laid dormant for thousands of years were put in soil, all of a sudden, they sprang up and produced.[4] That's powerful!

Parable of the Sower

And he said unto them, Know ye not this parable?
and how then will ye know all parables? The sower
soweth the word.

Mark 4:13–14

According to Jesus, the parable of the sower (Mark 4:1–20) is the key to unlocking all of God's Word. If we don't understand these truths, Jesus said we won't understand any of the other parables.

In this parable, Jesus described four types of soil into which seed could be sown, but He really wasn't teaching about agriculture. When Jesus later explained the parable to His disciples, He revealed that the seed was the Word of God and that the soil was people's hearts.

The variable in this parable is the condition of these hearts. God's Word is always the same. It has the same potential in every heart. As Jesus gave the parable, He described each kind of soil as it related to people's hearts. First, there was the ground by the wayside (Mark 4:4), then the stony ground (Mark 4:5–6), the seeds sown among thorns (Mark 4:7), and the good soil that yielded thirty-, sixty-, or a hundredfold (Mark 4:8).

A heart represented by the wayside ground is one that has no desire toward God's Word. The Word never gets inside of the heart but lays on the surface where it's easily stolen away by the devil. Jesus said that Satan has the ability to steal this Word from those who don't understand it (Matt. 13:19). Therefore, understanding is the first step in getting God's Word down on the inside of us.

This stony ground represents a person who understands God's Word and is excited about it but doesn't take the time to get it rooted inside (Mark 4:16–17). In that case, the Word does germinate, but it doesn't produce fruit because it doesn't have a good root system. Someone who isn't rooted in the Word of God will wither and fall away when persecution or criticism comes.

The third kind of soil concerns thorns choking out or restricting the ability of other plants to grow and produce fruit. This type of ground represents those who are distracted and deceived by worldly things (Mark 4:18–19). The Word sown in their hearts is choked, and no fruit is produced.

And other fell on good ground, and did yield fruit that sprang up and increased; and brought forth, some thirty, and some sixty, and some an hundred.

Mark 4:8

What made this fourth kind of soil good ground? Why did it yield fruit thirty-, sixty-, and a hundredfold? Did it have more than the other types of ground? No, it actually had less. It had fewer weeds to drain the nutrients. It also had less of a rocky base so the seed could put down roots. There was less of a threat to snatch the seed away. So, more soil isn't necessary for our hearts to be good ground. It just takes less occupation with the things of the world and more focus on the Lord.

Even among those who were fruitful, there were varying degrees of fruitfulness, but many people feel that they just don't have what it takes to become fruitful. But the truth is that any of us can see God's Word produce in our lives if we root out all the contrary things. Good ground doesn't just happen. It has to be cultivated.

The Earth Brings Forth

And God said, Let the earth bring forth grass, the herb yielding seed, and *the fruit tree yielding fruit after his kind, whose seed is in itself, upon the earth: and it was so.*

Genesis 1:11

Notice the verse says that the earth brought forth plants and trees. They were already in the earth and God brought all of these things—everything that we see—out of the ground with His Word. Did you know everything you see above ground was once in the ground? There are things all around us made of wood, plastic, glass, and metal that were once in the ground.

Even mankind was made out of the ground. Genesis 2:7 says,

*And the L*ORD *God formed man* of *the dust of the ground, and breathed into his nostrils the breath of life; and man became a living soul.*

When God created mankind, they were in the earth. His Word activated what was already in the ground—minerals, nutrients, etc.—and brought forth man. Then, the Lord breathed into us His breath. That's what made us different than any of the other creatures He brought forth from the earth and water in Genesis 1. So, we aren't just physical; we also have this spiritual part. That word *breath* is the same word that's also translated *spirit*.

When God spoke to the earth, it became the seed that released all that potential that was in the ground. Likewise, when you take the written Word of God and sow it in your heart, it becomes alive. The Word of God activates the life that's in your spirit and starts releasing it into the physical realm—through the fruit of the Spirit—healing, deliverance, prosperity, and other promises from His Word.

When you look in the mirror, you may see someone who isn't as gifted as somebody else. Maybe you feel like you missed out on all kinds of great talents. And while that may be true in the natural, your spirit man is identical to Jesus (1 John 4:17). You have everything in your born-again spirit that is in Jesus. All you need to do to activate it is by planting the seed of the Word of God in your heart, and it'll start drawing out the life of God.

One time at a meeting in Kansas City, a man came up and told me I was "plain as dirt." Now, I don't think he meant that as a compliment, but dirt is miraculous. What is in the ground—plain old dirt—has the potential to produce everything around us. That's awesome!

God Made Seed

And God said, Behold, I have given you every herb bearing seed, which is upon the face of all the earth, and every tree, in the which is the fruit of a tree yielding seed; to you it shall be for meat.

Genesis 1:29

The parable of the sower really isn't a parable about how to plant a seed and get a harvest in the natural sense. It's just a natural phenomenon used to illustrate a spiritual principle. It's appropriate that Jesus used this illustration for the Word of God because a seed is not man-made—it's God-made.

You could pool the entire resources of the human race—all of our money, intellect—and put billions of people to work at coming up with something that looks like a kernel of corn. It might taste like a kernel of corn, and it might even crunch like a kernel of corn. It could be like corn in every respect, but if you put a man-made kernel of corn in the ground, it would never produce a stalk, and it would never produce new ears of corn.

There is a miracle in a seed. When you plant a seed, it just produces. It multiplies thirty-, sixty-, or a hundredfold. And I believe it's very significant that God chose a seed to illustrate the way the Word works in your heart. Because if he used something man-made for his illustration, it just wouldn't be the same.

In school, students are taught and given tests, but they can cheat on a test. You could look at somebody else's paper and copy their answers. You could also sit in class, not pay attention, and not really absorb the material. In that case, the night before a test, you could cram the information in your short-term memory just to pass. In a sense, that is also cheating. You can circumvent the learning process and pass a test without really learning the material.

The vast majority of people have done that to some degree. If you tried to retake some of the tests that you took in high school, you probably couldn't pass them today. You may have passed them then, but you didn't retain the material. You didn't really learn it. You just beat the system. You can beat a man-made system, but you can't beat a God-created system. You can't cram for a harvest.

Know When to Sow

A man who attended a Bible study I led years ago was probably one of the worst sinners in that whole county. He was a drunk and a womanizer. Then he was miraculously born again and baptized in the Holy Spirit. Just as much as he had served the devil, he turned around and served God with all his heart.

Everybody in the county was aware of what had happened. He couldn't go anywhere—the post office, grocery store, or gas station—without people recognizing the transformation. Because of this, he had many opportunities to be a witness. This man started talking to everybody about the Lord and opened up his home so I could teach the Word. Sixty or seventy people were coming to that Bible study just to see the change in this man.

He had zeal for the Lord, but he made some serious mistakes because he didn't know the Word. He started traveling and giving his testimony on top of all he was doing in his church. Because of his busy schedule, he just didn't have time to plant his crops the way he normally did. This guy owned so much land that he counted it in sections. Each section was 640 acres.

Since he was serving the Lord, this man just assumed that God would supernaturally bless him with a crop even though he didn't take time to sow it. The wheat season progressed, and it was about three weeks or so before harvest. Other people's wheat was up, had started turning golden in color, and they were getting ready to reap. About that time, this man went out and borrowed $500,000 to buy wheat seed and planted it just days before the harvest.

He thought that God would grant him a supernatural harvest because he had been out doing "the Lord's work." Of course, this supernatural harvest didn't happen. When his wheat didn't grow up, and he didn't harvest it, he lost all that money. He was in jeopardy of going bankrupt. This man then came to me, wanting prayer.

He was angry, saying, "I don't understand why God didn't give me this harvest!" I had to tell him, "That isn't the way the kingdom works. You have to plant your seed at a certain time and give it time to grow and mature. These are just natural laws." He countered, saying, "I know that's the way it works. I've been doing this for years. But I thought that since I was in the Spirit that things would just work differently!"

This man was just verbalizing what many people think. They think in the natural realm that they're bound by these physical, natural laws, and certain things have to happen before expected results can come. But in the spiritual realm, they think that if they're sincere, really in need, and mean it with all of their heart, that they can expect positive results to come without preparation. That's not how it works.

Seed, Time, and Harvest

So is the kingdom of God, as if a man should cast seed into the ground; and should sleep, and rise night and day, and the seed should spring and grow up, he knoweth not how. For the earth bringeth forth fruit of herself; first the blade, then the ear, after that the full corn in the ear. But when the fruit is brought forth, immediately he putteth in the sickle, because the harvest is come.

Mark 4:26–29

In the natural world, everything revolves around seed, time, and harvest. It's the same in the spiritual world. God's Word is the seed that, given time, produces a harvest. But God just doesn't give you everything that you desire or need all at once. To some of you, it may feel like it's seed, **T I M E**, and harvest, but there is definitely a growth process. People who ignore this do so to their own detriment. It hurts you if you don't acknowledge this.

I remember a man who came to me with an idea for a youth center in Colorado Springs. He had heard a message about reaching out to youth, and it really got his attention. So, he found this empty retail building (one that I had also looked at for our ministry facilities), which would've cost about $2 million to purchase. Then he estimated it would cost another $2–$3 million to renovate.

This man was planning to put in a skate park and other features that would draw teenagers. While they were there, he would minister to them. It was a great idea, and he had put a lot of time and effort into creating a proposal that he brought to me, hoping I would endorse it. The proposal was full of facts and figures, talking about crime among youth and other things—to help justify the need for a Christian youth center in the city.

Then I started asking this man questions. "Have you ever taught a Bible study? Have you ever worked in a youth group? Have you ever dealt with youth?" And he answered, "No," each time. It turns out, he had never done any ministry work. So, I said, "It's a great idea, but it won't work for you."

"Why not?" he asked. And then he tried to justify his plans according to the need. He referred again to all the statistics in his proposal. I didn't dispute there was a need, but I told him, "You have never been used a little bit, so you aren't going to be used a lot. It's first the blade, then the ear, and then the full corn in the ear."

This man wanted all the fruit of a harvest without going through seed and time. God's will for your life doesn't come to pass automatically or even immediately. For you to go from zero to a thousand miles an hour instantly isn't acceleration—*it's a wreck!* There is a growth process.

Get Understanding

When any one heareth the word of the kingdom, and understandeth it not, then cometh the wicked one, and catcheth away that which was sown in his heart. This is he which received seed by the way side.

Matthew 13:19

Understanding is absolutely critical for the Word of God work in your life. While it's a good thing to speak the Word—because faith comes by hearing and hearing by the Word of God (Rom. 10:17)—you shouldn't just recite the Word without understanding what you're saying. There are some people who use the Word of God like a mantra, and it is unfruitful for them because they lack understanding.

I remember in one of my meetings, I was praying for a person who had some demonic problems, and those demons ended up manifesting. I had my eyes closed while I was praying, and people later told me this person was trying to hit me, but they just couldn't touch me. It was like somebody was stopping them, and I believe it was the Lord protecting me.

What I do remember, though, is that when this person started screaming, yelling, and trying to hit me, everyone around us started reciting the Lord's Prayer (Matt. 6:9–13) as fast as they could. Again, it's good to speak the Word to your situation, but these people were just reciting out of tradition—like when somebody does it in a movie to scare away a vampire. They weren't doing it with their understanding.

I'll tell you, the devil's not afraid of the Bible. (In fact, he may have even been involved in some of the modern translations!) He's also not afraid of tradition. Just reciting Bible verses isn't going to cast out a demon. It has to involve something more than just using your rosary beads, repeating some prayer over and over, or quoting some scripture.

> *Wisdom* is *the principal thing;* therefore *get wisdom: and with all thy getting get understanding.*
>
> Proverbs 4:7

You've got to understand the Word. It's got to be a part of you! You have to put the seed of God's Word in your heart and let it conceive. That's understanding! The only way you are truly going to see your life change and watch God's best just come out of your born-again spirit is to read and meditate on the Word and understand it.

I've had so many people come to me and say, "You just make the Word so simple to understand." Well, that's because I'm pretty simple! If a person is going to be an effective communicator, they've got to speak on a level that people can understand. If they don't understand it, Satan just comes immediately and steals it away. You've got to understand the Word of God before you can really receive it and see it produce.

Know When to Reap

Along with knowing when to sow and allowing time for things to mature, there is also a proper time to harvest. If you try to harvest too early, the fruit will be green, and it won't ripen. Basically, you will kill your harvest if you reap it too soon. Similarly, if you wait too long to harvest, it will die on the vine and begin to rot. There is a proper time to reap your harvest, and it takes just as much wisdom to know when to reap as it does to sow.

Learning how to harvest is something that took me a long time to figure out. I was good at planting the Word in my heart and it was producing, but I didn't always know how to reap. This is one of the things we tell students in our Charis Bible College. By sitting under the Word four hours a day, five days a week, their lives will change. They can also learn from the experiences of our instructors and not have to go through the "school of hard knocks" like I did.

Our ministry is dependent upon people giving and helping us. In the early days of our ministry, we struggled financially. I was ignorant of a law in the kingdom of God that says, *"the Lord ordained that they which preach the gospel should live of the gospel"* (1 Cor. 9:14). In other words, a minister's income is proportional to their preaching of the Gospel.

In the beginning of our ministry, I didn't understand this principle. I was only ministering in a small Bible study. In the first church I ever pastored, the largest crowd we had was twelve people, and most of the time, it was only five to seven people. When I was preaching part-time and only ministering to a few people, I should have only expected to reap a part-time salary. I should have been working to supplement it.

At the time, I didn't understand that. I personally felt like I was sinning against God if I went and worked a secular job because I was called into the ministry. So, because of that, Jamie and I nearly starved to death. Now, through television, the internet, books, and Charis, I minister to billions of people all over the world. God has supplied my needs from preaching of the Gospel.

There is an appropriate time to reap, and you can't reap if you aren't sowing. You can't make a withdrawal from a bank if you don't have anything deposited. In the early days, I wasn't sowing enough to live off preaching the Gospel. I couldn't expect people to support me unless I made a deposit in their lives. Nowadays, it's not unusual for me to send an appeal letter to our partners and friends for their help on a project and see a huge response. I'm reaping proportional to my sowing. That's a blessing!

Allow God's Word to Grow

And he said, Whereunto shall we liken the kingdom of God? or with what comparison shall we compare it? It is like a grain of mustard seed, which, when it is sown in the earth, is less than all the seeds that be in the earth: but when it is sown, it groweth up, and becometh greater than all herbs, and shooteth out great branches; so that the fowls of the air may lodge under the shadow of it.

Mark 4:30–32

When I served in the military in Vietnam, it would take two weeks for news to arrive from the United States. Years after I got home, I had the chance to meet astronaut Jim Irwin when we were being interviewed on the same television program. Afterword, I asked him a bunch of questions about landing on the moon because I was in Vietnam when a lot of those space missions happened.

Today, with television and the internet, we have a twenty-four-hour news cycle. It doesn't matter where you are in the world, you can be constantly bombarded with information as events happen. The news media works around the clock. They are not just reporting what is happening anymore. They are making projections and forecasting all kinds of tragedy. People open the door to fear through negative reports. But you have to sow the Word of God diligently if you want to see growth in the things of God.

When I first arrived in Vietnam, and I laid on my bunk and studied the Bible, I read Mark 4:30–32, which made a huge impact on me. I saw in this parable that the Lord was talking about growth, comparing it to a huge tree that spreads out until the birds of the air come and land in it. Jesus was saying that God sows a seed in your heart, and it grows. As it begins to produce, you begin ministering to other people and their lives are changed.

As I was reading this and praying, I said, "God, I want you to touch my life and use me so I can touch people all over the world." I had no idea I'd be reaching millions of people around the world through television and Charis Bible College, but I had the desire for it. So, I was just praying, "God, I want to be this huge tree that reaches out to touch and bless people."

And the Lord spoke to me and said, "If I were to answer your prayer today and give you this worldwide ministry that you desire, the first bird that landed on one of your branches would cause the whole thing to fall over because your root is about an inch deep." The Lord went on to tell me to not worry about the growth above ground but to put emphasis on getting rooted in the Word of God.

Put Down Roots

Blessed is *the man that walketh not in the counsel of the ungodly, nor standeth in the way of sinners, nor sitteth in the seat of the scornful. But his delight is in the law of the LORD; and in his law doth he meditate day and night. And he shall be like a tree planted by the rivers of water, that bringeth forth his fruit in his season; his leaf also shall not wither; and whatsoever he doeth shall prosper.*

Psalm 1:1–3

In this analogy, a tree was planted by the rivers of water, and its roots went down and tapped into a river so that even during a period of drought, it would still bring forth fruit. The tree would flourish because its root system tapped into subterranean moisture that would sustain it. In contrast, a tree that was just dependent upon the rain would die during a drought because its root system didn't have anything to draw on.

This describes so many Christians. They haven't put down their roots and tapped into a personal relationship with the Lord. They're just living off Sunday services, friends who pray for them, or something else. You've got to have deeper roots than that. There are so many people who want to see the visible things of God, but they aren't willing to spend time with the Lord and let their roots go down deep.

Years ago, a student from our Charis Bible College came up to me because they were just really touched by a message that I gave. They asked, "How long did it take you to prepare that message?" They were probably thinking it took an hour or two, but I said, "Thirty-two years." At the time, that's how long it had been since I had my miraculous encounter with the Lord on March 23, 1968. That message was something I had been living for thirty-two years.

Now, I've been living these truths I'm sharing with you for more than fifty years. I have spent so many hours meditating on the Word and building my relationship with the Lord, these things are just a part of me. It's rooted on the inside of me and, because of that, it's producing fruit in me and in other people through this ministry.

Maybe you desire some of the same results I have, but you don't have any root in you. You are not planted by a river. You don't know what the Word of God says. You may have heard someone else quote Scripture and you think, *Well, I know the Bible says somewhere that God wants me to be prosperous, healed, and delivered.* But you're not seeing God's best manifested in your life; you're not seeing fruit. You just have to get to where you know the Word of God better than that.

Choose Your Mold

And be not conformed to this world: but be ye transformed by the renewing of your mind, that ye may prove what is that good, and acceptable, and perfect, will of God.

Romans 12:2

While I served in the Army, I only heard one good thing from a chaplain the whole time I was there. Most of the chaplains I had weren't even born again. But the day we got our orders to go to Vietnam, there was a chaplain who really blessed me.

Once we got the news about going overseas, grown men began to cry. It was a tragic situation, and so this chaplain came in to console everybody. He said that the Army and its experiences, including Vietnam, would be a like a fire. "It will melt you," this chaplain said. "But you get to choose the mold you're poured into." What he said turned out to be a true statement.

Because I had already set my heart on the Lord, I was determined that I was going to go all the way for Him. All the pressures and the horror I went through drove me that much more toward Lord. So, when I came back from Vietnam, I was stronger than horseradish! I was walking with God, the joy of the Lord was in my heart, and I was a thousand miles further along in my Christian walk.

You may not be a soldier in the midst of a war zone, but you will still have pressures come against you in this life that will melt you. However, you can choose whether you'll be like the other people who become negative, bitter, and unforgiving. You can choose whether you'll murmur and complain or if you'll let these things drive you to the Lord and make you stronger and more stable in your commitment to Him.

In other words, it's your choice whether you become bitter or better. So how do you make that choice?

The Greek word rendered *transformed* In Romans 12:2 is *"metamorphoo."*[5] It's the word from which we derive our English word *metamorphosis*. A little caterpillar spins a cocoon and then, after time, turns into a beautiful butterfly. If you want to be transformed from something creepy, crawly, and earthbound into something beautiful that can fly, you need to be metamorphosed or transformed by the renewing of your mind.

Your life will change, one way or the other, but you get to choose whether it's negative or positive. Do you want to change from being weak, inferior, and bound by all kinds of problems into someone who releases and experiences the abundant life of God (John 10:10) from within? If so, you must renew your mind to the Word of God.

Every Idle Word

If we want to start seeing the power of God manifest in our lives, we will have to start paying attention to what we say. Words have power—more than any of us realize—but we often speak them as though they are meaningless. Because of that, most believers at one time or another have been hung by their tongue.

Matthew 12:36–37 says,

But I say unto you, That every idle word that men shall speak, they shall give account thereof in the day of judgment. For by thy words thou shalt be justified, and by thy words thou shalt be condemned.

"*Every idle word*" simply means "nonproductive." These are words that you speak but don't believe. For example, you might say, "I'm dying to see my grandchildren."

You really don't mean you're dying, but you say it anyway to emphasize the importance of the relationship.

> *For with the heart man believeth unto righteousness; and with the mouth confession is made unto salvation.*

Romans 10:10

Every time you say things that you don't really mean, it begins to numb your heart to God's Word. Each idle word is making it just a little bit harder to believe what you say will actually come to pass when you mean it and it really counts.

At the same time, Romans 10:17 says, *"faith* cometh *by hearing."* The words you speak are picked up by your own ears, so whatever you are saying is making faith come. Your faith is also affected by what someone else says, especially if they have a place of authority over you.

A good friend of mine once told me how his dad kept used cars for parts. They had lots of junk cars parked on their farm at any given time, and his dad would take parts out of one to repair something else. Every time my friend helped repair the cars, his dad would say, "You're so stupid! You can't screw a nut on a bolt without cross-threading it."

After years of hearing that message, it became a self-fulfilling prophecy in my friend's life. I remember working with him on a car. As smart and capable as my friend was, I'd watch him shake every time he had to put a nut on a bolt—terrified he'd cross-thread it. One time, my friend had put the nut on just fine, but he was so afraid that he had cross-threaded it, he took the nut off and put it on again. He kept doing it until eventually he did cross-thread that bolt. To this day, I've never seen my friend put a nut on a bolt that wasn't cross-threaded. He had been cursed by his father's words.

Holy Dissatisfaction

Delight thyself also in the LORD; and he shall give thee the desires of thine heart.

Psalm 37:4

Before you change, you've got to become dissatisfied with where you are. You need a holy dissatisfaction with your circumstances. It's one of the ways that God reveals how He is leading you.

I remember when Jamie and I were ministering in Seagoville, Texas. We never had a large group there. We struggled financially, and it was hard on us yet we stayed there for two years. I had friends who asked, "Why don't you leave this place? Why don't you go someplace where people want you?" But I just loved being in Seagoville.

I remember being at our church building one day and praying. When I looked out of the windows, it was as if everything I saw went from color to black and white. It went from being something that I liked to just being drab. I remember looking out of the windows and thinking, *This is the dinkiest town. Who would live in this place?*

All of a sudden, my love and my desire to be in Seagoville changed. It was so dramatic that I thought, *God, what's going on?* I prayed for about two hours. Eventually the Lord spoke to me and told me that on November 1, I was to leave Seagoville. At that time, God didn't tell me where I was supposed to go, but He just told me it was time for a change.

The way the Lord showed me was by changing my desires (Ps. 37:4). I didn't desire to be in Seagoville any longer. I knew that God wanted me to move on. But then I thought, *How am I going to break this to Jamie?* So, I prayed about it for a long time.

When I got home, there was a "For Sale" sign in our yard that wasn't there when I left earlier that day. I asked

Jamie, "What happened?" She said, "The landlord came by and said they're selling our house, and we've got to be out on November 1." That was the exact date that God had given me, and it was a confirmation. There was a change taking place in my life, and one of the ways that I discovered it was because I just knew in my spirit that there was something more.

It was during this time that I was sowing the Word into my heart. Even though I loved the people of Seagoville, I was delighting myself in the Lord first. Years before, I knew I would have a worldwide ministry, but the Lord showed me that I had to put roots down in my spirit by sowing the *"incorruptible seed"* (1 Pet. 2:23); I had to delight myself in Him.

Make a Change

By January 31, 2002, I had known for more than thirty years that God wanted me to reach people all over the world. I knew I was going to have a worldwide ministry, and I was moving in that direction, but I was just inching along. At the rate I was going, it probably wouldn't have happened in my lifetime. But when the Lord spoke to me and told me I was limiting Him by my small thinking, something happened. I made a decision to change. I was going to believe big.

I spent time meditating on what the Lord had shown me based on Psalm 78:41. Not only that, but I had also consistently sown God's Word in my heart for more than thirty years by that point. Because of this, I was able to draw out of my born-again spirit when I taught in our Bible college. In a sense, I had been preparing for this moment my entire adult life.

Through pastoring three small churches, broadcasting on radio, being a traveling minister, establishing Charis, and then being on television, we had seen, *"first the blade, then the ear, after that the full corn in the ear"* (Mark 4:28). By taking the limits off God and changing the way I was thinking, I was reaping the fruit produced by years of sowing seed. The change inside me had been happening effortlessly, and now it was time to change outwardly.

I'll tell you, it didn't take long to see the impact this had on our ministry. I sat down and wrote a letter to our partners, sharing what the Lord had shown me. Because printing and mailing takes time, along with our partners' responses, we didn't expect to see a change in their giving for months. But people started giving and our income increased almost instantly. That was before my letter reached our partners. It was supernatural!

At about the same time, we had a breakthrough with the second-largest Christian television network in America. I was friends with the people who operated it but for whatever reason, we just couldn't get on their network. Then one day, this couple contacted me and asked, "Why aren't you on our network?" Wouldn't you know it, our program was on there just one week later!

Our Bible school was so cramped that we converted all of the inside restrooms to ladies' rooms and made all of the guys use portable toilets outside, even during the winter. We eventually found a building that was 110,000 square feet and the Lord showed me how we could convert it all into offices and classroom space without going into debt. Our partners gave us more than $3 million, and within fourteen months we had moved into that new building. It was awesome!

Through the years, God has continued to show me that I need to keep changing the image on the inside of me. I truly believe until the day I go to be with the Lord, He's going to be showing me that there's more to believe for— there's more I can do. And with Him, all things are possible!

Conclusion

Many of you have dreams and visions from God, and you would love to do something different. Yet, you're afraid to step out and try. You need to overcome this fear of change. There is a way to change without it being traumatic, painful, or laborious. There is a right and a wrong way to change. God's way to change is from the inside out by sowing His Word into your born-again spirit.

People say they want to change, but they get frustrated when they don't see results right away. Part of the reason is because we live in an instant society. People can get fast food at the drive through, or they get irritated when they can't connect to the internet right away. Well, you can't just microwave your miracle.

Growth doesn't just happen all at once. There is first the blade, then the ear, and then the full corn in the ear. There are always steps to the fulfillment of a vision or word from God. Those who haven't taken baby steps will never take great steps. But all you've got to do to start seeing God's perfect will for your life come to pass is to just take the seed of God's Word and plant it in your heart, and your heart will automatically bring it to pass.

I truly believe that if you meditate in the Word day and night (Josh. 1:8), if you don't let the devil steal it from you (Mark 4:15), and don't let the cares of this life choke out your growth (Mark 4:19), I believe you would have to backslide on God to keep from fulfilling His perfect will for your life.

You need to recognize that God wants you to change. He made you for more than what you are experiencing. Most people are shooting at nothing and hitting it every time. That's not the way that God made us to be.

If you just let God's Word work in your heart and allow it to bear fruit, you will see change for the better. Through God's principle of seed, time, and harvest, your life will have to change, and it will just happen effortlessly!

FURTHER STUDY

If you enjoyed this booklet and would like to learn more about some of the things I've shared, I suggest my teachings:

- *Spirit, Soul & Body*
- *Plain as Dirt*
- *You've Already Got It!*
- *God Wants You Well*
- *Don't Limit God*
- *The Heart of Man*

These teachings are available for free at **awmi.net**, or they can be purchased at **awmi.net/store**.

Receive Jesus as Your Savior

Choosing to receive Jesus Christ as your Lord and Savior is the most important decision you'll ever make!

God's Word promises, *"That if thou shalt confess with thy mouth the Lord Jesus, and shalt believe in thine heart that God hath raised him from the dead, thou shalt be saved. For with the heart man believeth unto righteousness; and with the mouth confession is made unto salvation"* (Rom. 10:9–10). *"For whosoever shall call upon the name of the Lord shall be saved"* (Rom. 10:13). By His grace, God has already done everything to provide salvation. Your part is simply to believe and receive.

Pray out loud: "Jesus, I acknowledge that I've sinned and need to receive what you did for the forgiveness of my sins. I confess that You are my Lord and Savior. I believe in my heart that God raised You from the dead. By faith in Your Word, I receive salvation now. Thank You for saving me."

The very moment you commit your life to Jesus Christ, the truth of His Word instantly comes to pass in your spirit. Now that you're born again, there's a brand-new you!

Please contact us and let us know that you've prayed to receive Jesus as your Savior. We'd like to send you some free materials to help you on your new journey. Call our Helpline: **719-635-1111** (available 24 hours a day, seven days a week) to speak to a staff member who is here to help you understand and grow in your new relationship with the Lord.

Welcome to your new life!

Receive the Holy Spirit

As His child, your loving heavenly Father wants to give you the supernatural power you need to live a new life. *"For every one that asketh receiveth; and he that seeketh findeth; and to him that knocketh it shall be opened…how much more shall* your *heavenly Father give the Holy Spirit to them that ask him?"* (Luke 11:10–13).

All you have to do is ask, believe, and receive! Pray this: "Father, I recognize my need for Your power to live a new life. Please fill me with Your Holy Spirit. By faith, I receive it right now. Thank You for baptizing me. Holy Spirit, You are welcome in my life."

Some syllables from a language you don't recognize will rise up from your heart to your mouth (1 Cor. 14:14). As you speak them out loud by faith, you're releasing

51

God's power from within and building yourself up in the spirit (1 Cor. 14:4). You can do this whenever and wherever you like.

It doesn't really matter whether you felt anything or not when you prayed to receive the Lord and His Spirit. If you believed in your heart that you received, then God's Word promises you did. *"Therefore I say unto you, What things soever ye desire, when ye pray, believe that ye receive them, and ye shall have them"* (Mark 11:24). God always honors His Word—believe it!

We would like to rejoice with you, pray with you, and answer any questions to help you understand more fully what has taken place in your life!

Please contact us to let us know that you've prayed to be filled with the Holy Spirit and to request the book *The New You & the Holy Spirit*. This book will explain in more detail about the benefits of being filled with the Holy Spirit and speaking in tongues. Call our Helpline: **719-635-1111** (available 24 hours a day, seven days a week).

Endnotes

1. *The Strongest Strong's Exhaustive Concordance of the Bible*, 21st Century ed. (2001) s.v. "αὐτόματος" ("automatos").

2. *Blue Letter Bible*, s.v. "σπορά" ("spora"). Accessed August 18, 2023, https://www.blueletterbible.org/lexicon/g4701/kjv/tr/0-1/.

3. *Blue Letter Bible*, s.v. "σπέρμα" ("sperma"). Accessed August 18, 2023, https://www.blueletterbible.org/lexicon/g4690/kjv/tr/0-1/.

4. Laura Clark, "Tree Grown From 2,000-Year-Old Seed Has Reproduced," *Smithsonian Magazine*, March 26, 2015. Accessed August 18, 2023, https://www.smithsonianmag.com/smart-news/tree-grown-2000-year-old-seed-has-reproduced-180954746/.

5. *Blue Letter Bible*, s.v. "μεταμορφόω" ("metamorphoō"). Accessed August 18, 2023, https://www.blueletterbible.org/lexicon/g3339/kjv/tr/0-1/.

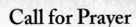

Call for Prayer

If you need prayer for any reason, you can call our Helpline, 24 hours a day, seven days a week at **719-635-1111**. A trained prayer minister will answer your call and pray with you.

Every day, we receive testimonies of healings and other miracles from our Helpline, and we are ministering God's nearly-too-good-to-be-true message of the Gospel to more people than ever. So, I encourage you to call today!

About the Author

Andrew Wommack's life was forever changed the moment he encountered the supernatural love of God on March 23, 1968. As a renowned Bible teacher and author, Andrew has made it his mission to change the way the world sees God.

Andrew's vision is to go as far and deep with the Gospel as possible. His message goes far through the *Gospel Truth* television program, which is available to over half the world's population. The message goes deep through discipleship at Charis Bible College, headquartered in Woodland Park, Colorado. Founded in 1994, Charis has campuses across the United States and around the globe.

Andrew also has an extensive library of teaching materials in print, audio, and video. More than 200,000 hours of free teachings can be accessed at **awmi.net**.

Contact Information

Andrew Wommack Ministries, Inc.

PO Box 3333
Colorado Springs, CO 80934-3333
info@awmi.net
awmi.net

Helpline: 719-635-1111 (available 24/7)

Charis Bible College

info@charisbiblecollege.org
844-360-9577
CharisBibleCollege.org

For a complete list of all of our offices,
visit **awmi.net/contact-us**.

Connect with us on social media.